A Ladybird
Easy-Reading Book
Series 606G

This book gives a colourful glimpse of Denmark and its many islands. It shows some of the interesting things you can see in that country, and how the Danish people live and work.

A LADYBIRD 'EASY-READING' BOOK

come to DENMARK

by IRENE DARK

with illustrations by JOHN BERRY

Publishers: Wills & Hepworth Ltd Loughborough

First published 1971   ©   *Printed in England*

COME TO DENMARK

If you were to travel to Denmark by aeroplane and look out of the window, you would see that Denmark is a land of many islands as well as one large peninsula, called Jutland.

The islands appear like pieces of a jigsaw thrown on to a blue cloth. The largest are Zealand, Fyn, Lolland, Langeland, Falster, Mön and Bornholm.

You will find that wherever you go in Denmark, you are not far from the sea. Because of this, the Danes have developed a very efficient system of water transport between the islands.

There are some bridges, like the one in the picture, linking islands, but transport is mainly by boat. Sometimes there are so many boats sailing between Zealand and Fyn, across the water called *The Great Belt*, that they look like one continuous stream each way. They carry passengers, freight, cars and trains.

0 7214 0288 7

Copenhagen, the beautiful capital city of Denmark, is on the island of Zealand. The different shapes of the buildings, towers and spires make the skyline of the city very attractive. It is often called 'the city of beautiful spires'.

One magnificent spire is on the Stock Exchange (or Bourse, as it is called). It is made of the twisted tails of four copper dragons. Another interesting spire has a spiral staircase running round the outside of it. On the top is a golden ball with the figure of a man above. In the lovely Town Centre Square you will see the City Hall with its warm-coloured, red brick walls and tower, and copper spire.

With canals, like the one shown opposite, running through the city and with the harbour alongside, Copenhagen seems almost like a seaside holiday town.

As you walk around Copenhagen you will notice bicycles everywhere. Everyone seems to be riding a bicycle. This is because the roads are not too hilly in any part of Denmark.

At Gammel Strand, the fish market, you will see the fishermen's wives in national costume, serving customers with fish. At fishmonger's shops you will see fish swimming around in the tanks until purchased. This means they are really fresh. The customer selects the fish she wants, and the fishmonger catches it, kills it and cleans it ready for cooking.

Much of the fish caught by the thousands of fishing boats all round the coasts is sent to factories. Here it is either canned, filleted or smoked. It is then sold in Denmark or to other countries.

Most people in Copenhagen live in flats instead of houses. These are very pleasant, often with balconies but no gardens. Instead you will see window-boxes, full of gay flowers.

Many of these flat dwellers have a little house of their own in a Garden Colony. Garden colonies are made up of little chalet houses like the one in the picture, each with a small garden where a family can enjoy the sun and fresh air every weekend in summer. Each little chalet flies the Danish flag when the family is 'in residence'.

When holiday time comes, many of the town children go off to camp. Special trains leave the big Central Railway Station, carrying hundreds of children, with their teachers, to farms or school camps. Friends and onlookers all give them a send-off.

One of the things you will remember most about your stay in Denmark will be your visit to the Tivoli Gardens in Copenhagen. This really is a fairyland, where you can choose to do just what you like. You can enjoy a trip on a small motor boat on the lake, a ride in a goat cart, or an exciting trip on the starlike Ferris Wheel which carries you high into the sky so that you can see all Copenhagen.

Orchestras play, and there is a Pantomime Theatre and a Fun Fair.

You may see and hear the 'Tivoli Boy Guards' as they march around the Gardens looking like 'toy soldiers'.

When evening comes, everywhere is lit with coloured lights. Fountains glow and sparkle as they leap up into the dark sky, and at midnight fireworks light up the lake in a wonderful display before everyone goes home.

In Denmark there is a Royal Family. If you stand outside the royal residence at twelve o'clock midday, you can see the Changing of the Guard.

When the King is in residence, the Life-Guards wear blue uniforms and tall, fur helmets made of bearskin. On the King's birthday they wear a red uniform. The people of Copenhagen seem to like bright colours. Postmen wear bright red uniforms, customs men wear blue, and the chimney sweeps wear top hats!

The Danes care especially for those who are not strong, or are old. You will notice as you walk around that some people are wearing armbands of yellow. These are the people who are blind or deaf. Drivers take extra care when they see these yellow armbands.

The Old People's City is a part many people like to visit, for here can be seen how well old people are cared for in Denmark. They have pleasant rooms and beautiful surroundings.

Along the promenade, called *Langelinie*, is the beautiful statue of 'The Little Mermaid'. This was placed there as a memorial to Hans Christian Andersen, who wrote many of our favourite fairy stories.

The Little Mermaid was a character in one of Hans Andersen's fairy tales, a mermaid who looked longingly out to sea, hoping for the return of her lover.

Across the harbour the cranes and buildings of the great shipyards can be seen, while in the harbour many ships are coming and going to other islands and lands.

Denmark is famous for its crafts, especially silverware, woodwork, stoneware, glass and china.

It is possible to visit the factories and watch these lovely things being made.

The Royal Copenhagen Porcelain Factory is a wonderful place to see. It is in a wooded park with avenues and canals. Here a guide will take you round and show you how vases, jugs, bowls and figurines are made. Some of the figurines are made up of quite small pieces which are put together so that no join can be seen.

Artists work at painting the articles, studying real flowers, models or pictures so that the details are right. When the articles are finished, they are glazed, put into a kiln to be 'fired' and then cooled off. They are then ready for sale all over the world. Many people make a hobby of collecting them because of their beauty and value.

A trip to Odense, on the island of Fyn, (or Funen), seems to take us right into storyland, for here Hans Christian Andersen was born. The little yellow house which you see in the picture is there, and inside are many interesting things to see. You can also see the school to which he went.

In the country round about Odense are many of the places which inspired fairy tales —towns with timbered houses; narrow, quaint streets; harbours; soft, round hills; orchards and pretty villages with old cottages. It is even possible to see storks, and their untidy nests, on the chimneys of the houses.

The Manor House, the cottage, the moat and even the swans which inspired 'The Ugly Duckling' story can still be seen.

It is indeed a fairytale countryside.

In Denmark there are many small farms, each one usually belonging to a family. Each member of the family helps on the farm. Pigs, cows and poultry are kept, and wheat, rye, barley, oats, root crops, grass and clover are grown. Because crops are grown *and* animals kept, the farms are called 'mixed farms'.

Most farmers are members of several co-operative undertakings, and between them own their dairy factories and bacon factories.

Every morning a milk lorry calls for the milk. This is taken to the Creamery and tested. The skimmed milk (that which is left when the cream is taken) goes back to the farm for feeding pigs. The cream is made into butter and cheese which is packed for export in factories like the one shown opposite. Much of this can be seen in our supermarkets and grocer's shops.

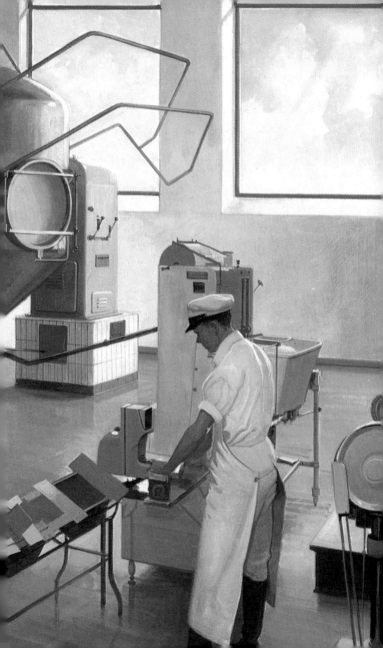

The poultry from the farms goes to large factories. There the birds are killed, de-feathered and packed into big refrigerators before being sent to the shops or to other countries. The feathers from these birds are sent to a factory for making into feather beds. Danish people not only sleep on feather mattresses, they also sleep with a feather quilt over them.

When the pigs are fully grown, they are taken to bacon factories. Danish bacon is some of the best in the world. You can see the word 'Danish' on this bacon when it is in the shops of countries outside Denmark.

Each farmer produces most of the food for his cows and pigs. Each person working on a Danish farm produces enough food for about eighty-five people.

In Denmark land is scarce and every inch is used. It is cultivated right to the edge of a road or river, with no space for a hedge.

Because of this, you will often see cows feeding in a long line across the field instead of wandering on their own. Sometimes they are tethered to a stake, or an electric fence is used to keep them to a particular part of a field. In this way none of the grass is wasted.

All along the north-west coast of Jutland are long stretches of sand and sand dunes. In the south, some of the sandy area is being reclaimed from the sea, so that it can become farmland. Long 'dykes' are built to hold back the sea, and the sea-water behind them is pumped out.

In many places the sandy beaches are so firm and wide that not only are they ideal bathing beaches, but motor cars can drive along them—and even light aircraft can land.

Denmark has some fascinating castles. Kronborg Castle, with its green, copper roofs above yellow stone walls, and its copper towers topped with golden balls, was built to protect the waters around Elsinore. Now it is a museum of ships and history.

Down below are big, dark dungeons, and on the courtyard walls are old cannons.

Not far away are two more beautiful castles. One of them, Fredensborg, is set in wonderful parkland. The other, Frederiksborg Palace, is a large, red-walled castle with many spires, gold balls, weathercocks and statues. You have to cross a number of bridges in the terraced gardens to reach the castle.

In the picture opposite you will see Egeskov Castle, in Fyn (or Funen). It is built in a lake and the only way in is over a draw-bridge. Inside you can see many secret passages and hiding places.

Jutland is the largest part of Denmark. It is a peninsula and not an island.

The old cathedral in Aarhus is the longest in Europe and very beautiful. Most visitors enjoy the 'Old Town', which is really an open-air museum. Here there are lovely, old squares, alleys and streets. Some of the houses overhang a stream. Old houses which would otherwise have been demolished, have been brought here from other towns and re-erected. Inside you will see that they are furnished just as they used to be. One really feels one is walking through a town of the past.

Another town, Ebeltoft, has crooked cobbled streets, old houses and a tiny Town Hall, guarded by cannons. It seems like a toy town.

Skagerak and Kattegat are the names given to the waters between Denmark and Norway and Sweden.

Here the north-west winds blow strongly and lifeboatmen have a busy time, for the finger-like spit of sand called Grenen seems to move with the direction of the wind or tide. Then ships are likely to run aground.

Esbjerg, on the west coast is a big and important port for fishing and trading. Its fleet of trawlers in harbour, and its nets hanging out to dry are a fascinating sight, telling just how important a fishing port this is. Passengers by boat from Britain to Denmark land at Esbjerg.

All Danish towns are a mixture of old and new. At Aalborg in Jutland, the cathedral, the castle, the town hall and the monastery are all very old buildings.

Jens Bang's famous old trading house, shown opposite, is a tall, six-storey building with decorated gables around its steep roof. In olden times the traders and merchants went there to talk business.

In the main street in Aalborg, you will see a statue of a goose girl holding a goose. Out of its bill water is pouring into a fountain. This reminds us of Hans Christian Andersen's fairy tale, 'The Goose Girl'. In the city the big statue of a charging bull is called 'The Cimbrian Bull' and is in memory of the Danish tribe, the Cimbrians, who marched on Rome, hundreds of years ago.

Aalborg is a centre for exploring North Jutland. If you take a trip to 'The Skaw', or 'The Tip', you can stand with one foot in the North Sea and one foot in the Kattegat.

Bornholm is called 'The Holiday Island'. It has a long, warm, sunny season. Bornholm is a night's journey by ship from Copenhagen, and is about the size of the Isle of Man.

Here there is something for everyone. You can choose cliff climbing, sunbathing on sandy beaches, watching the white fishing boats, visiting a smoked herring factory, picking mushrooms or exploring old buildings.

The queerly-shaped rocks have names like Candlerock and Lion's Heads. The singing of the nightingales in the woods is one of the chief delights of Bornholm.

Four round churches, high and built of rough granite, white-washed and with tiled roofs, remind you of the days when they were also fortresses. Pirates and enemies often invaded the island. Then the villagers took refuge inside the round churches.

Herrings are very good to eat, and Bornholm is especially famous for its 'Bornholmere' herrings.

The fishing boats come in every morning laden with their catch. It is very interesting to watch the women working on the catch. They cut and clean out the fish, wash them and hang them up in pairs by piercing and fixing them together by the heads, over wooden bars.

Here the fish are left to dry in the air. Then the bars of herrings are carried into the smoking house, where they are dried and smoked over fires built up of alder wood.

When they are a lovely, golden yellow, they are packed into boxes and sent by ship to Copenhagen. From there they are shipped to many other countries, as well as to the markets of Denmark.

Danish people love butter. Their favourite food is called 'Smorrebrod' which really means 'buttered bread'. We might call it a sandwich without a lid, for on top of the buttered bread is spread a most delicious selection of foods.

Here is a description of one selection: dark brown ryebread thickly spread with butter; on top, one slice of Danish liverpâté; a few slices of mushrooms fried in butter; one gherkin; one rasher of crisply fried bacon; one slice of tomato; one lettuce leaf. A knife and fork are needed to eat it. Such meals can be hot, but are usually cold.

At some restaurants, and usually only on Sundays, there are tables with a great variety of foods from which to choose. These tables are called 'cold tables', even though some of the several dozen dishes are hot! Opposite you can see what one of these tables might look like.

The money used in Denmark consists of krone and øre. A krone is worth about five new pence of our money.

There are 10, 50, 100 and 500 kroner notes, and coins of 1, 2, 5, 10 and 25 øre and 1, 2 and 5 kroner.

If you have a ten-kroner note, take a careful look at it. On one side is a picture of Hans Christian Andersen, and on the other is a countryside picture, with a farmhouse and a windmill similar to the one opposite. This is a real scene from Denmark, a land of windmills.

The paper money is made at a large paper-mill at Silkeborg. There you can see how wood pulp and rags are made into paper.

Machines looking like huge steam-rollers press the wet pulp out into thin, wafer-like sheets. The finished paper comes out in big rolls.

Silkeborg is a town that grew around the paper-mill. Now it is also a centre for holidays among lakes, hills, rivers and woods.

All over Denmark there are Folk High Schools where people can go to study. They are for adults, because the Danes are very keen to learn, to discover things and to get to know more about the land in which they live.

Here too, they meet, make friends and enjoy themselves. They can choose subjects in which they are most interested, such as art, history, poetry, folk-singing and folk-dancing.

At festival times they put on their beautiful national costumes. Then they dance traditional folk dances in towns and villages. Both the dances and the costumes are part of ancient Danish history.

Lace for these costumes is handmade. You can see the lacemakers at work in South Jutland. In Tönder, lacemaking has been carried on for centuries and is world-famous for its delicacy and fine workmanship.

A visit to one of the breweries makes a very interesting excursion. Both the Carlsberg and Tuborg breweries are in Copenhagen. They are world-famous for their beers and soft drinks.

At a brewery you will be welcomed and taken round the brew-house, the malt-house, the fermenting cellars, the bottling departments, the storage cellars and the despatch departments. Much of the up-to-date machinery is automatic and can be worked by one man.

The Tuborg brewery has its own harbour where boats are loaded with the cases of beer and soft drinks that go all over the world. Out in the streets of Copenhagen you will notice the gay, decorated brewery carts and horses.

All the profits of these two breweries are used to support art and science.

The Danes depend very much on trade with other countries. The goods that come into a country are called imports, and have to be paid for. The goods that go out to be sold to other countries are called exports. The sale of exported goods brings in money. Denmark, like other countries, wants to have more exports than imports.

Beside the export of butter, bacon, cheese, poultry and other produce from the land, Denmark has large industries which also export machinery, furniture, china, stainless steel goods, jewellery and ships. Much of the raw material, such as steel, has to be imported first. Important industries are the building of ships and the construction of ships' engines. To-day, one third of the diesel ships in the world have engines built in Denmark or made elsewhere by permission of the Danes.

Many miles away from Copenhagen, in the North Atlantic, is a group of islands, called the Faroe Islands. These islands, and also the large island called Greenland, belong to Denmark. The people who live and work there are also Danish citizens.

There, in summer, the nights are nearly as light as the days.

Up-to-date fishing trawlers go out from Greenland in all weathers to catch the fish for the factories on the islands. The sea around Greenland is often frozen, and three-quarters of the land is covered by a two-mile thick ice-cap. In the north there are polar bears, caribou and musk-oxen.

Look at a map to see where these islands are.